*To my mum, and all my
birdwatcher friends
who took me around.*

– N.T.

magnificent
BIRDS

ILLUSTRATED BY NARISA TOGO

WALKER ❙ STUDIO
AN IMPRINT OF WALKER BOOKS

Bald Eagle

Haliaeetus leucocephalus | NATIVE TO NORTH AMERICA

In some North American cultures, the majestic bald eagle has long been regarded as sacred. The bird appears in many creation stories representing values of strength and courage, and its feathers have symbolic meaning. The Lakota people wish peace and happiness by waving a feather over a person's head, while Navajo people use the eagle's feathers to celebrate an accomplishment or to protect themselves. As the only eagle native solely to North America, the bald eagle was chosen by the founders of the United States in 1782 to be the country's national bird.

Spectacular flight displays are performed by the bald eagle both to defend territory and to reinforce a bond with their mate. A pair will swoop, soar and cartwheel before locking talons and free-falling until they almost hit the earth. From its hunting grounds over lakes and coasts, the eagle returns to the same nest every year. Usually about five-feet wide and four-feet deep, the nests can grow much bigger as pairs add to them each year until the supporting branches snap under the increasing weight.

andean flamingo

Phoenicoparrus andinus | NATIVE TO SOUTH AMERICA

High up in the salt lakes of the Andes Mountains, huge flocks of pink Andean flamingos gather every summer to perform their courtship dance. Groups of males march and shuffle in tight formation, turning their heads quickly from side to side in a movement known as flagging, flicking their neck back to preen their feathers and gabbling and honking. This striking display is all designed to attract a mate; once a flamingo has a partner, they will stay together and care for one egg every year.

Though monogamous, flamingos are sociable and live in large flocks. One species found in Africa can gather in groups of more than a million birds. Flamingos' naturally grey plumage is transformed to bright pink by the food they eat. Andean flamingos fly hundreds of kilometres in a single day to find the right shallow, salty lake with the algae they prefer. Species of flamingos are found in Africa, the Middle East and the Caribbean, as well as South America.

greater bird-of-paradise

Paradisaea apoda | NATIVE TO INDONESIA AND PAPUA NEW GUINEA

In the rainforests of Papua New Guinea, Indonesia and Australia lives a family of birds with unusual and often beautiful plumage. Known as birds-of-paradise, the males of the 39 known species go to great lengths to attract a mate through elaborate displays. Some, such as the Wilson's bird-of-paradise, show off bright primary colours on their feathers and skin. Others, such as the ribbon-tailed astrapia, have incredible ornamental feathers that can be nearly a metre long. Many birds-of-paradise inherit a sequence of dance steps they display to impress females.

The greater bird-of-paradise is the largest of the family, at around 43 centimetres in length. In the rainforest canopy, the male calls and waits for a female to enter its courting territory. Often another male will display alongside it in competition. Once a potential mate is watching, the bird will parade and hop back and forth, shaking and showing off the extravagant feathers on its back. It will then freeze in a pose, allowing the female to inspect its plume. Such a display can last for hours.

japanese crane

Grus japonensis | NATIVE TO CHINA, RUSSIA, KOREA AND JAPAN

Also known as the red-crowned crane after the bare patch of coloured skin on its head, the Japanese crane is one of the rarest birds in the world. It is regarded as sacred and a symbol of luck and longevity in some parts of Asia, due to its loyalty to its partner. Japanese cranes usually mate for life and regularly perform a beautiful and elaborate dance with their partner to reinforce their bond. The pair will bow, throw their heads back and leap into the air, flapping their long wings.

Though it will roost in groups, the Japanese crane tends to forage for fish, rice and plants either alone or just with its partner or family. There are thought to be only 3,000 Japanese cranes left in the world, as its wetland homes dry up and fires destroy its nesting grounds. Where it survives, it has a lifespan of around 40 years in the wild. In Japan, however, the crane is known as the *tanchōzuru* and is said to live for 1,000 years.

common KINGFISHER

Alcedo atthis | NATIVE TO EURASIA AND NORTH AFRICA

A fast and efficient hunter, the kingfisher's success at snatching prey from the stream or river where it lives is due to its ability to use two types of vision. Many birds have eyes on the side of their heads and so use monocular vision (both eyes working separately), while birds of prey tend to have eyes at the front and use binocular vision (both eyes working together). When it dives, the kingfisher switches from monocular vision in the air to binocular vision in the water. By using both, it can judge the distance of its prey with deadly accuracy and overcome the challenges of hunting in water.

The kingfisher mostly eats small fish, but will swoop for aquatic insects and amphibians too. To sustain its whirring wingbeats and rapid flight, it needs to eat over half its bodyweight each day. The kingfisher will leave its burrow in the riverbank to perch on a branch above the water. There it waits, until it spots movement below and plunges after it in a characteristic flash of bright blue plumage.

toco toucan

Ramphastos toco | NATIVE TO SOUTH AMERICA

The toucan's large and colourful beak is instantly recognizable, but people have long been confused by what the bird uses it for. Growing up to twenty centimetres long, it can be nearly a third of the toucan's body length. Despite this, it is surprisingly lightweight, as it is made from keratin (the same material as human nails and hair) and filled with air pockets. For this reason it's unlikely the toucan can use its beak as a weapon. It has been observed using it to peel fruit and to play catch using scraps of food with a potential mate. It is also thought that the toucan can regulate its body temperature by adjusting how much blood reaches the beak's surface.

The toco is the largest of all toucans, and over double the size of the smallest, the lettered araçari. Living in flocks of about six, toco toucans nest in the hollows of trees and are not very adept at flying, preferring to hop between branches. They lay between two and four eggs each year, and both parents stay to care for their young.

RUBY-THROATED HUMMINGBIRD

Archilochus colubris | NATIVE TO NORTH AND CENTRAL AMERICA

During courtship, the wings of the male ruby-throated hummingbird move faster than the wings of any other bird. As it displays to a female, the male hummingbird reaches an incredible 200 wingbeats per second – nearly four times faster than its usual 53 beats. Hummingbird wings are connected to the body only at their shoulder joint, meaning they are able to rotate in a similar way to insects' wings. No other bird has wings like this and it is why the hummingbird can hover and fly so acrobatically.

Such rapid movement means the hummingbird may eat twice its bodyweight in a day to find enough energy, feeding mainly on nectar and sap, using its long tongue to probe flowers, but also eating insects and spiders. It has one of the highest metabolic rates of any animal; hummingbird hearts can beat over 1,000 times a minute. Only the female cares for the offspring. It builds a tiny, cupped nest out of grasses and spider webs, and camouflages it with dead leaves.

Bar-Tailed Godwit

Limosa lapponica | RANGES FROM ARCTIC TO AUSTRALIA AND NEW ZEALAND

To spend winter in Australia and New Zealand, the bar-tailed godwit makes the furthest non-stop flight of any bird. Flying over 11,000 kilometres across the vast Pacific Ocean from its breeding grounds in the Arctic, a flock of godwits can be in the air for around eight days. During its epic journey, the godwit doesn't eat but burns through fat reserves, losing more than half of its bodyweight. It will also shrink any organs it doesn't need in flight in order to reduce its weight and conserve energy. The godwit navigates by the sun and stars and rests by shutting down half its brain at a time.

When they return to the Arctic in the spring, the godwits take a longer coastal route and stop to feed at estuaries on the coast of the Yellow Sea. This is to make sure they have enough reserves for the breeding season. The godwit will forage in marshes and mudflats for insects, worms and crustaceans, competing with other members of the flock to store up enough energy for the rest of their relentless journey.

wandering albatross

Diomedea exulans | RANGES ACROSS SOUTHERN OCEAN AND NORTH PACIFIC

The wandering albatross has the largest wingspan of any living bird, measuring up to three and a half metres across. Though it spends most of its life in flight, it does not use its huge wings primarily for flapping, as this would use too much energy. Instead it uses a technique known as dynamic soaring, gliding up and down on ocean winds to generate momentum. In this way the albatross can be in the air for hours and travel vast distances without once flapping its wings. An albatross can cover thousands of kilometres in a single journey, and some have been known to circumnavigate the globe in only 46 days.

The wandering albatross holds a deep-rooted place in maritime lore as a symbol of good luck. Its significance to sailors likely stems from it following ships in search of food. Seldom seen on land, the albatross only comes ashore to breed on remote islands. Pairs mate for life and each year take turns to care for a single egg. Once a young albatross has its flight plumage, which develops before it is a year old, it spends the next five to ten years at sea, until it is ready to mate. Thought to be able to live for up to 50 years, the wandering albatross is one of the few birds that usually dies of old age, although modern fishing techniques are an increasing threat.

AUSTRALIAN PELICAN

Pelecanus conspicillatus | NATIVE TO AUSTRALIA, NEW GUINEA AND INDONESIA

The Australian pelican's eye-catching bill is the longest of any bird. It measures around 50 centimetres, and the elastic throat pouch that hangs from it can stretch to hold as much as eleven litres of water. The pouch is not, however, used to store food or liquid. Instead it is an effective and sensitive tool for catching fish, detecting them in murky water where the pelican cannot see. Once a fish is trapped in the pouch, the pelican presses its bill to its chest to drain the water, then swallows its catch whole. Often Australian pelicans will hunt in large groups, sometimes of more than 1,000 birds.

Though big and heavy, the Australian pelican is very buoyant, thanks to air sacs under its skin and in its bones. Like other large birds, it soars on thermals rather than flapping its long wings when flying, allowing it to cover hundreds of kilometres quite easily. Pelicans nest in flocks on wetlands and waterways. Each female lays two or three eggs in shallow bowls in earth or sand, but the nest can be a brutal place for the young. The first-hatched chick is often the only one to survive; usually the largest, it is given the most food by its parents and may kill its siblings.

barn owl

Tyto alba | WORLDWIDE

The near-silent flight of the barn owl in the night sky is only part of what makes it such a deadly hunter. Its sense of hearing is thought to be more sensitive than any other animal in the world. Although it hunts mainly at dawn and dusk, the barn owl is able to catch prey in total darkness from sound alone. A heart-shaped face that collects sound and one ear sitting higher than the other helps the owl to work out where a noise is coming from with pinpoint accuracy. It can also rely on its sharp eyesight, which is twice as sensitive as human sight.

The barn owl will swallow prey whole, then regurgitate inedible fur and bone in a compact pellet. When raising young with a female, with whom it will mate for life, the male owl brings extra food back to be shared among its owlets. By ten weeks, young barn owls will have mastered flying and can begin learning to hunt. Despite this parental care, as many as three quarters of barn owls die in their first year, with nearly half of hatchlings never making it out of the nest. A shortage of food is the most common cause.

emperor penguin

Aptenodytes forsteri | NATIVE TO ANTARCTICA

In the frozen Antarctic, where the temperature can drop to -60°C, extraordinary parenting is needed to keep emperor penguin chicks alive. Once the female has laid her egg, she passes care of it to the male and leaves to hunt. She often has to travel many kilometres to reach the edge of the ice pack and her ocean hunting grounds, where she is able to dive deeper than any other bird – over 500 metres – to catch fish, krill and squid.

While she is away the male balances the egg on his feet, protecting it from the elements under a brood pouch and huddling with other penguins to conserve heat. For two months, the male eats nothing, and may lose almost half his bodyweight. When the chick hatches, its father can produce a kind of milk from his oesophagus to feed it. When the female returns, she regurgitates food for the chick and takes over its care, leaving the male free to hunt. Once the chick is old enough to survive outside the brood pouch it joins a crèche of up to several thousand other juveniles. Eventually the whole colony will trek to the ocean together.

kakapo

Strigops habroptila | NATIVE TO NEW ZEALAND

Though they have lived in New Zealand since prehistoric times and are able to live to 90 years old, there are only three small islands in the Pacific Ocean where the kakapo, one of the rarest birds in the world, survives today. By the 1970s new predators such as feral cats meant that only eighteen male kakapos were thought to be left in the world. The species looked doomed to extinction until a small population of both males and females was found and an intensive conservation programme began. The kakapos were moved to protected islands, where they were supplied with food and closely monitored. Through this painstaking work, the kakapo population has now reached over 100.

Though it is a type of parrot, the kakapo is much larger than other parrots, climbs instead of flies, and only emerges from its nest on the ground at night. The kakapo is also the only parrot to have a "lek" breeding system, where groups of males gather to compete for females. The male digs a bowl on high ground to act as an amplifier, then, using its thoracic sac, inflates like a balloon and makes a sonic boom that can be heard from up to five kilometres away. It can perform like this for eight hours without a break, interspersing its booms with high-frequency "ching" sounds that pinpoint its location to any interested female.

peregrine falcon

Falco peregrinus | WIDESPREAD

The peregrine falcon is the fastest animal in the world. When it dives to capture prey in a movement known as a stoop, it can reach over 300 kilometres per hour. The falcon achieves such an incredible speed by having powerful flight muscles and by being efficiently streamlined. Its pointed wings and stiff feathers cut through the air with little resistance. To enable it to breathe at double the speed other birds can cope with, special bones above the falcon's nostrils direct airflow away, keeping the air pressure at a safe level.

Fittingly, peregrine means "wanderer", as it is found all over the world. Recently it has become a more common sight in cities, drawn by skyscrapers that mimic the cliff faces where the peregrine usually nests and an abundance of prey such as pigeons. On cliffs and buildings, young falcons are raised in shallow bowls scratched into dirt, and generations of falcons often use the same nesting sites for hundreds of years.

N A R I S A   T O G O is a printmaker and illustrator with a lifelong
love of birds. After receiving a Bachelor's degree in Ecology from the
Tokyo University of Agriculture and Technology, she completed a Masters
in Children's Book Illustration at the Cambridge School of Art. When she is
not in her studio producing the intricate reduction lino-cut artwork featured
in *Magnificent Birds*, Narisa takes groups birdwatching. She lives in Japan.

T H E   R S P B is the largest nature conservation charity in Britain.
Formed over 120 years ago, the RSPB works to provide a home for nature
and protect species from decline. It has more than a million members.

First published 2017 by Walker Studio, an imprint of Walker Books Ltd, 87 Vauxhall Walk, London SE11 5HJ
in association with the RSPB, The Lodge, Potton Road, Sandy, Bedfordshire, SG19 2DL
2 4 6 8 10 9 7 5 3 1
Text © 2017 Walker Books Ltd Illustrations © 2017 Narisa Togo
The right of Narisa Togo to be identified as illustrator of this work has been asserted by her in accordance
with the Copyright, Designs and Patents Act 1988. This book has been typeset in Avenir Next
Printed in China
All rights reserved.
British Library Cataloguing in Publication Data is available.
ISBN 978-1-4063-7788-0
www.walkerstudio.com

Published under licence from RSPB Sales Ltd to raise awareness of the Royal Society for the Protection of Birds
(Charity registration England and Wales no 207076, Scotland SC037654). For all items sold Walker Books will donate
a minimum of 6% of sales income received for this book to RSPB Sales Ltd, the trading subsidiary of the RSPB.
All subsequent sellers of this book are not commercial participants for the purpose of Part II of the Charities Act 1992.
www.rspb.org.uk
The RSPB logo is a registered trademark of the Royal Society for the Protection of Birds.